First World War
and Army of Occupation
War Diary
France, Belgium and Germany

52 DIVISION
Divisional Troops
Northumberland Fusiliers
17th Battalion (N.E.R. Pioneers)
1 June 1918 - 30 April 1919

WO95/2893/5

Published by

The Naval & Military Press Ltd

Unit 10 Ridgewood Industrial Park,

Uckfield, East Sussex,

TN22 5QE England

Tel: +44 (0) 1825 749494

www.naval-military-press.com

www.nmarchive.com

This diary has been reprinted in facsimile from the original. Any imperfections are inevitably reproduced and the quality may fall short of modern type and cartographic standards.

© **Crown Copyright**
Images reproduced by permission of The National Archives, London, England, 2015.

Contents

Document type	Place/Title	Date From	Date To
Heading	WO95/2893-5		
Heading	52nd Division 17th Bn Numberland Fus (Pioneers) Jun 1918 Apr 1919 From 32 Div Troops.		
War Diary		01/06/1918	30/06/1918
Miscellaneous	Headquarters 52nd Division "A"	02/08/1918	02/08/1918
War Diary	Neuville St Vast	01/07/1918	23/07/1918
War Diary	Tangry	23/07/1918	01/08/1918
War Diary	Ecurie	03/08/1918	03/08/1918
War Diary	Estree-Cauchie	17/08/1918	17/08/1918
War Diary	Tilloy	21/08/1918	21/08/1918
War Diary	Blaireville	23/08/1918	23/08/1918
War Diary	S.2.3+2	24/08/1918	24/08/1918
War Diary	M.36+T.1	26/08/1918	30/08/1918
War Diary	Sheet 57b SW M.36.+T.1	31/08/1918	31/08/1918
Miscellaneous	17th Bn. Northumberland Fusiliers Appendix		
War Diary	Sheet 57 C N.E.	01/10/1918	06/10/1918
War Diary	57c N.W.	07/10/1918	07/10/1918
War Diary	51c	08/10/1918	14/10/1918
War Diary	51b N.W.	14/10/1918	15/10/1918
War Diary	38c	16/10/1918	25/10/1918
War Diary	Sheet 44	26/10/1918	10/11/1918
War Diary	Sheet 45	11/11/1918	31/01/1919
Miscellaneous	Headquarters 52nd Division	02/03/1919	02/03/1919
War Diary	Sheet 45	01/02/1919	31/03/1919
War Diary	Sheet 38	01/04/1919	30/04/1919
War Diary	Soignies	01/04/1919	30/04/1919

woof/2ga5/2ge3(5)

woof/5ga5/2ga3/2ge3(5)

52ND DIVISION

17TH BN N'UMBERLAND FUS
(PIONEERS)
JUN 1918-APR 1919

From 32 Div
Troops

Army Form C. 2118.

17 N Fus

WAR DIARY
or
INTELLIGENCE SUMMARY
(Erase heading not required.)

Place	Date	Hour	Summary of Events and Information	Remarks and references to Appendices
France – MARROEUIL	1/6/18		SHEET A.3,5,5.2. Battn billeted in CELLAR CAMP, NEUVILLE ST. VAAST. (less "A" Co at VILLERS AUX BOIS). Working on shelter. Pipe line & improvement in trench. "A" Coy working on Erection of huts at Batt HQ.	G.S.O.
	2nd June		"D" Coy proceeded to live in dugouts in VILLERVAL SECTOR OF TRENCHES. Relieved by	G.S.O.
	9th June		"C" Coy. Working on front line repair. Returned to CELLAR CAMP 13th June.	G.S.O.
	16th June		"A" Coy concentrated at Batt. HQ.	
	11th June		Outbreak of P.U.O. (trench fever). Spread rapidly over 300 men sick at one time total eventually sick – 514 in all.	G.S.O.
	30th June		Orders to convert Battn from a Battn of Railway Troops to a Pioneer Battn. and posted to 32nd Division received.	G.S.O.
			Casualties: 1. O.R. died of Wounds. 2. O.R. died of Sickness. 4. O.R. Wounded. 2. O.R. Wounded (at duty).	

G.S. Gordon.
Captain & Adjutant.
For O.C. 17th (S) Bn Northd Fusiliers

Headquarters,
    52nd Division, "A"

       Herewith War Diary of this Unit for the month of JULY 1918.

2-8-1918.   Commdg. 17th Northumerland Fusiliers (N.E.R. Pioneers)

for Lieut. Colonel,

Vol 32

Place	Date	Hour	Summary of Events and Information	Remarks and references to Appendices
NEVILLE ST. VAST	July 1–23.		Batt? working on field defences; moved to: —	
TANGRY	July 23–31.		Batt? in training. Rifle shooting etc. Gasmasks in billets.	
			Casualties for July.	
			1. O.R. died of wounds.	
			1. O.R. wounded.	
			1. O.R. " (at duty).	

G.S. Gordon
Captain + adjt
17th North? Fus.

2/9/1918

Army Form C. 2118.

Page 1.

17th Northd. Fus.

WAR DIARY
or
INTELLIGENCE SUMMARY
(Erase heading not required.)

Place	Date	Hour	Summary of Events and Information	Remarks and references to Appendices
TANGRY	1/8/18	—	In billets. Batt undergoing training	G.S.G
ECURIE	3/8/18	—	Moved ½ Batt by Rail: ½ Batt (by Road (Lorries) to ECURIE. Batt employed on trench works — Reserve line + C.T. Moved to ESTREE-CAUCHIE by March route on 17th inst.	G.S.G
ESTREE-CAUCHIE	17/8/18		In billets. Batt. undergoing training. Moved night 20/21 by march route to TILLOY	G.S.G
TILLOY	21/8/18		Standing by to move into the line. Moved night 22/23 by march route to BLAIREVILLE QUARRIES.	G.S.G
BLAIREVILLE	23/8/18		Batt. employed on cutting trench for assembly in No Mans Land (1 Coy) " " improving roads + tracks for Artillery-troops (2 Coys) forward after the attack. Coys moved out to neighbourhood of BRICKSTACKS (Sheet 51f SW S.2.b+d.) on 24/8/18 Advanced H.Q. to same place — Batt. H.Q. at BLAIREVILLE.	G.S.G
S.2.b+d.	24/8/18		Coys working on Artillery roads + tracks following up the advance of the 52nd Div.	G.S.G
M.36+T.1	26/8/18		Adv. C.W. Hd. + Coys moved forward with Transport to M.36 + T.1. area Bivouaced in Trenches + working the bye, in neighbourhood of HENIN — SR-CUVOL towards CROISILLES. Divisn + Batts. relieved 27/8/18 night + Concentrate in bivouac in neighbourhood MERCATEL to rest.	G.S.G
M.36+T.1	29/8/18 → 30/8/18		Coys working on Roads + Tramway Stns. Same area as before.	G.S.G

33(2)

WAR DIARY or INTELLIGENCE SUMMARY

(Erase heading not required.)

Army Form C. 2118.

Page 2.

17 N F

9/8 33

Place	Date	Hour	Summary of Events and Information	Remarks and references to Appendices
Sheet 57 B S.W. M.36 → T.I.	31/8/18		Batt. H.Q. moved to T.21.d.7.8. Companies working as before (previously reported wounded in July)	Y.S.C.
			Casualties August 1918. Killed – 1 died of wounds – 1 wounded – 10 at duty. 8.	

Geo. S. Curson
Captain & Adjt.
for OC 17th North'd Fus. (Pioneers)

17TH BN. NORTHUMBERLAND FUSILIERS.

1918.   **Appendix.**

September.

1st.	Batt. H.Q. at T.21.d.7.8. Companies in Bivouacs near MERCATEL. working on improvement of tracks S.E.	51.B.S.W. 51.B.S.E.
2nd.	B.Coy. moved to U.20.c.9.5. Battalion working on roads near ST. LEGER and CROISILLES.	57.C.N.W.
3rd.	A.Coy. moved to B.6.a.9.6. B. Coy. moved to C.6.d.5.9. - C. Coy moved to D.1.a. Battn. working on track BULLECOURT - QUEANT and making new Div. H.Q.	57.C.N.E.
4th.	A.Coy. moved to D.7.a.6.7. owing to camp being shelled.	
7th.	Battn. H.Q. moved to T.4.b.5.3. A.Coy moved to B.10.d.5.5. B. Coy moved to C.1.d.8.6. C.Coy moved to B.9.a.8.5. Transport moved to U.19.c.2.8. Battn. working on road ST.LEGER - ECOUST.	
12th.	B.Coy. moved to D.1.a.5.0. On work on new Division H.Q. "A" and "C" on road as before.	
16th.	Battn. H.Q. moved to D.7.6.7.0. A. Coy to D.7.d.3.8. C. Coy to V.19.c.5.1. - Battn. employed on roads QUEANT - PRONVILLE also on consolidating fanx front line near MOEVRES.	
17th.	T/Major MARTIN, G.W. Killed near PRONVILLE. 2nd/Lieut. G.McKAY Wounded.	
27th.	Companies moved to vicinity of BOURSIES to bivouac prior to attack on 27th inst. During 27th Companies working on Canal du Nord.Crossings which were made passable for guns and Infantry by evening. Adv. Bn. H.Q. formed D.21.d.	
28th.	Companies improving Canal crossings - Ditto on 29th inst.	
30th.	Companies salvaging arms &c. on area near MOEUVRES.	

           Casualties.   Killed 1 Officer   7. O.R.
                         Wounded 2 Officers 21 O.R.
                         Died of Wounds 1   O.R.
                         Wounded (at duty) 1. O.R.

           (Sgd) G. D. GORDON. Capt. & Adjt.
                         17th N.F.

17TH BN. NORTHUMBERLAND FUSILIERS.

P/52

1.

1918.   Appendix.

September.

Date		Appendix
1st.	Batt. H.Q. at T.21.d.7.8. Companies in Bivouacs near MERCATEL. working on improvement of tracks S.E.	51.B.S.W. 51.B.S.E.
2nd.	B.Coy. moved to U.20.c.9.5. Battalion working on roads near ST. LEGER and CROISILLES.	57.C.N.W.
3rd.	A.Coy. moved to B.6.a.9.6. B. Coy. moved to C.6.d.5.9. - C. Coy moved to D.1.a. Battn. working on track BULLECOURT - QUEANT and making new Div. H.Q.	57.C.N.E.
4th.	A.Coy. moved to D.7.a.6.7. owing to camp being shelled.	
7th.	Battn. H.Q. moved to T.4.b.5.3. A.Coy moved to B.10.d.5.5. B. Coy moved to C.1.d.8.6. C.Coy moved to B.9.a.8.5. Transport moved to U.19.c.2.8. Battn. working on road ST.LEGER - ECOUST.	
12th.	B.Coy. moved to D.1.a.5.0. On work on new Division H.Q. "A" and "C" on road as before.	
16th.	Battn. H.Q. moved to D.7.6.7.0. A. Coy to D.7.d.3.8. C. Coy to V.19.c.5.1. - Battn. employed on roads QUEANT - FRONVILLE also on consolidating front line near MOEUVRES.	
17th.	T/Major MARTIN, G.W. Killed near FRONVILLE. 2nd/Lieut. G.McKAY Wounded.	
27th.	Companies moved to vicinity of BOURSIES to bivouac prior to attack on 27th inst. During 27th Companies working on Canal du Nord.Crossings which were made passable for guns and Infantry by evening. Adv. Bn. H.Q. formed D.21.d.	
28th.	Companies improving Canal crossings - Ditto on 29th inst.	
30th.	Companies salvaging arms &c. on area near MOEUVRES.	

Casualties.   Killed 1 Officer 7. O.R.
                Wounded 2 Officers 21 O.R.
                Died of Wounds 1 O.R.
                Wounded (at duty) 1. O.R.

                (Sgd) G. D. GORDON. Capt. & Adjt.
                        17th N.F.

Army Form C. 2118

WAR DIARY
INTELLIGENCE SUMMARY

17th Batt. Norfolk Regt.

October 1918   Page 1

(Erase heading not required.)

Instructions regarding War Diaries and Intelligence Summaries are contained in F.S. Regs, Part II. and the Staff Manual respectively. Title Pages will be prepared in manuscript.

Place	Date	Hour	Summary of Events and Information	Remarks and references to Appendices
Shet 57C N.E.	1st		Batt. H.Q. moved from D.7.b.7.0. to E.28.d.2.4. and Coys moved to K.4.4.4 and K.5.a.4.c. A & B Coys moved to F.28.a.4.c and C Coy to F.26.b.. All Coys working on roads in forward area.	L
"	2nd		All Coys working on roads and communication trenches.	L
"	3rd to 5th			L
"	6th		Batt. moved to J.8.	L
57C N.W.	7th		Batt. personnel entrained at VAULX-VRAUCOURT. Transport proceeded by Route march to BRETENCOURT.	L
51C	8th		Batt. personnel arrived TINQUES ad 0100, detrained and proceeded to MANIN by march route leaving 0400. Transport proceeded to MANIN by march route arriving 1630	L
"	9th to 13th		In billets — Battalion training	L
"	14th		Transport moved by march route to ECURIE. Orders received that Batt. would work under CE VIII Corps.	L
57C N.W.	15th		" " " IZEL-LES-ESQUERCHIN. Batt. personnel moved by march route to IZEL-LES-ESQUERCHIN	L
38C	16th 17th 18th		Bus to FRESNES-LES-MONTAUBAN and then by march route to IZEL — ROUVROY road. Coys working on IZEL — ROUVROY road.	L
"	19th		B. Coy moved to LAUWIN-PLANQUE on 18th. H.Q. Transport and A. Coy moved to LAUWIN-PLANQUE, C. Coy moved to DOUAI. A & B Coys working on IZEL — AUBY road.	L
"	20th		A. Coy moved to DOUAI. B. Coy working on IZEL — AUBY road, C. Coy working with	L

WAR DIARY
INTELLIGENCE SUMMARY

17th Batt. Monk'd Fus.

October 1918. Page 2

Place	Date	Hour	Summary of Events and Information	Remarks and references to Appendices
Sheet 1 38c	21st		R.E. on heavy bridges in DOUAI. B Coy working on roads, A & C on heavy bridges.	
	22nd		H.Q, Transport and B Coy moved to RACHES. A & C Coy working on heavy bridges in DOUAI.	
	23rd 24th 25th		B Coy working on roads, A & C Coy on heavy bridges.	
	25th		Coys working with R.E. on heavy bridges.	
Sheet 44	26th		A Coy moved to SARS-ET-ROSIERS. B & C Coys working on heavy bridges.	
"	27th		A Coy working on ORCHIES — ST AMAND road. B & C Coys on bridges.	
"	28th		H.Q. & Transport moved to BOUVIGNIES. A Coy working on roads, C Coy on bridges.	
"	29th		B Coy moved to LECELLES I.36.c.7.2. A Coy " " " C Coy " "	
"	30th		B Coy working on roads in forward areas. A Coy " " C Coy " "	
"	31st		H.Q. & Transport moved to VIEUX CONDE H.24.b. B Coy working on roads in forward areas. C Coy moved to BOUVIGNIES. Battalion assumed road duties of 52nd DIVISION on night 29th/30th.	

CASUALTIES OCTOBER 1918:-

KILLED 3 O.R.
WOUNDED 13 O.R.
WOUNDED AT DUTY 3 O.R. Gaetamii Cpl.

a/Adj. for O.C. 17th M.F.

WAR DIARY or **INTELLIGENCE SUMMARY** 17th Northumberland Fusiliers

Army Form C. 2118.

November 1918 Page 1.

Place	Date	Hour	Summary of Events and Information	Remarks and references to Appendices
Sheet 44	1		Batt. H.Q. Venus Cnodl' H.24.b.1.2.. A Coy moved to Berthinguaine and C Coy to Rue-Caston 1.24... Coys working on roads in divisional area.	
	2		B Coy moved to Pont du Jour. 1.36.C.. Coys working on roads in divisional area. 1.26.D.	
	3&4		Coys working on tools and salvaging timber in funnel avenue.	
	5		B Coy moved to la CROISETTE P.10.D. Coys working as on 3rd.	
	6		" " " " "	
	7		A Coy moved to PONT du JOUR 1.36.C.	
	8		Batt H.Q moved to MONT du ROY J.28.c.19. A Coy moved to Q.2.8. and worked on road approaches to bridges over flooded area in K.33.. B Coy moved to Q.3.8 and worked on roads in funnel avenue. C Coy moved to HAUTE RIVE J.30.C. and worked on road approaches to bridges.	
	9		Batt H.Q. moved to PERUWELZ L.2.a.7.9... A&C Coys working as on 8th. B Coy moved to PERUWELZ L.2.d.	
	10		C Coy moved to GRANDGLIS G.6.C. d.b.1.4.5. A Coy working as on 8th. B Coy working on roads in vicinity of PERUWELZ	
Sheet 44 5	11		Batt H.Q. moved to SIRAULT I.1.C.1.6. A Coy moved to le HARPART H.4... B&C Coys working on roads.	
	12		B Coy moved to VILLEROT H.19. and C Coy to BAUDOUR I.16.b.Coys working on roads.	

WAR DIARY or INTELLIGENCE SUMMARY

Army Form C. 2118.

17th Northumberland Fusiliers

November 1918 Page 2

Place	Date	Hour	Summary of Events and Information	Remarks and references to Appendices
Sheet 45	13		C Coy moved to VACRESSE C.30.c. Coys working on roads	
	14 to 18		Coys working on roads.	
	19		Batt. H.Q. moved to CHATEAU MONFORT J.33.b. Coys working on roads	
	20		A Coy moved to GHLIN J.27.b. " "	
	21 to 25		Coys working on roads and pack horse training.	
	26		Battalion moved to MASNUY-ST-JEAN O.18 & E.13. HQ at O.18.a.9.1.	
	27 to 30		Battalion training	
			Casualties nil.	

J. D. Gowrie Capt. a/a/a/4y
for O.C. 17th N.F.

Army Form C. 2118

DECEMBER 1918.

17th NORTHUMBERLAND FUSILIERS

WAR DIARY
or
INTELLIGENCE SUMMARY
(Erase heading not required.)

Instructions regarding War Diaries and Intelligence Summaries are contained in F. S. Regs., Part II. and the Staff Manual respectively. Title Pages will be prepared in manuscript.

Place	Date	Hour	Summary of Events and Information	Remarks and references to Appendices
Sheet 44/N A5	1/12/18		Battalion in billets at MASNUY-ST-JEAN. Coys. training - Military Educational and Recreational.	Vol 31/4
	2/12/18		Casualties - Nil.	

2119

Jas Garvie
Capt & Adjt
for O.C. 17 Northd Fus.
(N.F.R. Pioneers)

36(1)

Army Form C. 2118

WAR DIARY
or
INTELLIGENCE SUMMARY
(Erase heading not required.)

17th ̶(̶A̶r̶m̶y̶)̶ Northumberland Fusiliers (N.F.R.) January 1919

Place	Date	Hour	Summary of Events and Information	Remarks and references to Appendices
Sheet 45.	1/1/19 to 17/1/19		Battalion in billets at MASNUY ST. JEAN. Companies training - Military, Educational and Recreational.	
	18/1/19		Battalion attended Divisional Ceremonial Parade at MAISIERES at which the XXII Corps Commander presented Military Crosses and Distinguished Conduct Medals to Officers and men of the Division.	
	19/1/19 to 26/1/19		Battalion in billets at MASNUY ST. JEAN. Companies training - Military, Educational and Recreational.	
	27/1/19		Battalion Ceremonial Parade at JURBISE. XXII Corps Commander Lieut: General Sir A.J.GODLEY, K.C.B., K.C.M.G., presented the King's Colour to the Battalion on behalf of His Majesty the King. Lieut. E.R.WILKINSON received the Colours.	
	28/1/19 to 31/1/19		Battalion in billets at MASNUY ST. JEAN. Companies training - Military, Educational and Recreational.	

Headquarters,
    52nd. Division.
    ————————

                                    CONFIDENTIAL.

> 17th (S) BATTALION
> NORTHUMBERLAND FUS.
> (N.E. RAILWAY PIONEERS).
>
> No. 6/13
> Date 2/3/19

            War Diary for the month of February is enclosed
herewith, please.

                            J R Ladler
                        Commanding,   Captain,
2nd. March 1919.   17th. Bn. Northumberland Fusiliers
                                        (NER Pioneers).

WAR DIARY 17th. Bn. Northumberland Fusiliers Army Form C. 2118
(NER Pioneers).

INTELLIGENCE SUMMARY

(Erase heading not required.)

Instructions regarding War Diaries and Intelligence Summaries are contained in F.S. Regs., Part II. and the Staff Manual respectively. Title Pages will be prepared in manuscript.

Place	Date	Hour	Summary of Events and Information	Remarks and references to Appendices
Sheet 45	1/2/1919 to 5/2/19.		Battalion in Billets at Masnuy St.Jean. Companies training - Military, Educational and Recreational	
	6/2/1919		Divisional Boxing Finals - 17/731 Pte E.W. Soulsby wins the "Heavies" and Light-heavies" 17/1246 Pte F.Quinney wins the "Welters" and 17/1469 Pte C.Anderson obtains second place in the "Feathers".	
	7/2/1919		Battalion team wins the 52nd. Divisional Cross Country Run	
	8/2/1919 to 14/2/19.		Battalion in Billets at Masnuy St.Jean. Companies training - Military, Educational and Recreational.	
	15/2/1919.		Battalion team represents 52nd. Division in XXII Corps Cross Country Run and wins. Draft of 10 officers and 76 other Ranks proceed to join the 36th. Bn. Northumberland Fusiliers.	
	16/2/1919 to 28/2/19.		Battalion in Billets at Masnuy St.Jean. Training ceased as the strength of the Battalion is so low owing to Demobilisation. *discontinued*	

Captain,
Commanding, 17th. Bn. Northumberland Fusiliers (NER Pioneers).

WAR DIARY 17th Northumberland Fusiliers, (N.E.R.Pioneers).

or

INTELLIGENCE SUMMARY

(Erase heading not required.)

Army Form C. 2118

Vol 40

39(1)

Place	Date	Hour	Summary of Events and Information	Remarks and references to Appendices
Sheet 45	1/3/1919 to 20/3/1919		Battalion in Billets at Masnuy ST. JEAN. Checking of Stores and Equipment is carried out	
	20/3/1919		Battalion moved by march route to SOIGNIES	
	21/3/1919 to 31/3/1919		Battalion in Billets at Soignies, Checking of Stores and equipment completed.	

J. Sadler
Captain and Adjutant,
17th Northumberland Fusiliers,(N.E.R.Pioneers.)

Army Form C. 2118

WAR DIARY
or
INTELLIGENCE SUMMARY

(Erase heading not required.)

Instructions regarding War Diaries and Intelligence Summaries are contained in F.S. Regs., Part II. and the Staff Manual respectively. Title Pages will be prepared in manuscript.

Place	Date	Hour	Summary of Events and Information	Remarks and references to Appendices
SHEET 38 SOIGNIES.	1/4/19 to 30/4/19		Battalion in billets at Soignies, recieving demobilization stores.	

Lieut, A/Adj,
17th Northumberland Fusiliers,(N.E.R.Pioneers)

www.ingramcontent.com/pod-product-compliance
Lightning Source LLC
Chambersburg PA
CBHW081509160426
43193CB00014B/2630